I0794977

NEWSMAKERS

CHARLES III

KING OF THE UNITED KINGDOM

BY TAMMY GAGNE

Core Library
An Imprint of Abdo Publishing
abdobooks.com

Cover image: King Charles leaves the London Clinic in January 2024.

abdobooks.com

Published by Abdo Publishing, a division of ABDO, PO Box 398166, Minneapolis, Minnesota 55439.

Printed in the United States of America, North Mankato, Minnesota.
102024
012025

THIS BOOK CONTAINS RECYCLED MATERIALS

Cover Photo: Max Mumby/Indigo/Getty Images Entertainment/Getty Images
Interior Photos: Samir Hussein/WireImage/Getty Images, 4–5, 36, 45; Aaron Chown/WPA/Getty Images News/Getty Images, 8; Fox Photos/Hulton Archive/Hulton Royals Collection/Getty Images, 10; Evening Standard/Hulton Royals Collection/Getty Images, 12–13; William Vanderson/Fox Photos/Hulton Royals Collection/Getty Images, 15, 43; Hulton-Deutsch Collection/Corbis Historical/Getty Images, 18–19; Serge Lemoine/Hulton Archive/Hulton Royals Collection/Getty Images, 20; UPI/Bettmann Archive/Getty Images, 22; Bettmann/Getty Images, 26–27; Keystone/Hulton Archive/Hulton Royals Collection/Getty Images, 29; Shutterstock Images, 30 (crown); Red Line Editorial, 30 (succession line), 41; Hugo Bernand/ROTA/Anwar Hussein Collection/Getty Images News/Getty Images, 34–35; Jane Barlow/AFP/Getty Images, 39

Editor: Kari Cornell
Series Designer: Marley Richmond

Library of Congress Control Number: 2024938380

Publisher's Cataloging-in-Publication Data

Names: Gagne, Tammy, author.
Title: Charles III: King of the United Kingdom / by Tammy Gagne
Other title: King of the United Kingdom
Description: Minneapolis, Minnesota: ABDO Publishing, 2025 | Series: Newsmakers | Includes online resources and index.
Identifiers: ISBN 9781098295691 (lib. bdg.) | ISBN 9798384916697 (ebook)
Subjects: LCSH: Charles III, King of Great Britain, 1948---Juvenile literature. | Kings and rulers--Biography--Juvenile literature. | Monarchs--Biography--Juvenile literature. | Royalty--Biography--Juvenile literature. | Great Britain--Juvenile literature.
Classification: DDC 941.086--dc23

CONTENTS

CHAPTER ONE

ASCENDING THE THRONE

On May 6, 2023, 74-year-old Charles III was crowned King of England at Westminster Abbey. He was the oldest monarch in British history to take the throne. Charles had attended his mother's coronation in this same church 70 years earlier. Now it was his turn to swear the oath to become the new monarch. He had spent most of his life preparing for this day.

Charles's family was there to celebrate the occasion. His wife, Camilla, became queen. Both of the king's sons, Prince

King Charles III and Queen Camilla greeted the British people from the balcony at Buckingham Palace after his coronation.

William and Prince Harry, were also in attendance. In addition to these and many other family members, more than 2,200 people from more than 200 countries filled the church to witness the historic event. Another 18.8 million people watched the coronation on television.

Near the end of the ceremony, the Archbishop of Canterbury placed the St. Edward's Crown on Charles's head. The crown was crafted for King Charles II in 1661. Every monarch since then has been crowned with it. Charles was the fortieth monarch to be crowned at Westminster Abbey. And he likely will not be the last. Charles's oldest son, William, is next in line to someday ascend the throne.

WHAT IT MEANS TO BE KING

The United Kingdom is a constitutional monarchy. This means the king or queen works with Parliament, which is the governing body of the nation. Under this system, the role of the monarch is mostly symbolic.

King Charles III is not supposed to choose sides in politics.

The king has many duties as monarch. He regularly meets with the United Kingdom's prime minister at Buckingham Palace. These conversations are private. But they are believed to focus on state affairs and government policies. The king is also the person who officially appoints new prime ministers. Although voters elect the prime minister, the monarch leads the ceremony to make the appointment official.

CHANGING TIMES

People in the United Kingdom are divided about having a monarchy. Many older citizens remain supportive of having a king or queen. They believe the monarchy is part of British culture and tradition. But others think that royalty is an outdated concept. Less than 14 percent of British citizens under 35 years of age think it is very important for their country to have a monarchy. Some people spoke out against spending so much money on the coronation when there were Britons struggling to get by.

King Charles and Prime Minister Rishi Sunak met at Buckingham Palace after Sunak's election to the office in October 2022.

Charles also meets with leaders from around the world to promote good relations between the United Kingdom and other nations. He hosts many dinners and other formal events. The king also attends numerous charity events. His job involves a great deal of travel. During his first year as king, Charles visited many countries, including France, Germany, and Kenya. Charity work and travel were not new to Charles. As a member of the royal family, he had been performing these types of duties for most of his life.

A PRINCE IS BORN

Prince Charles Philip Arthur George was born on November 14, 1948, at Buckingham Palace. News of his arrival spread quickly through the United Kingdom. Charles was the first child of Princess Elizabeth and Philip, Duke of Edinburgh. The couple welcomed their daughter, Anne, in 1950. Charles was second in line to the throne. Elizabeth, the daughter of King George VI, was first in line at this time. People throughout the United Kingdom

A BIG DECISION

King George VI became king in 1936 when his brother, Edward VIII, abdicated the throne. Edward wanted to marry Wallis Simpson. But royals were not allowed to marry someone who had been divorced, as Simpson had been. If Edward hadn't stepped down, it is unlikely that either Elizabeth or Charles would have ascended the throne.

Prince Charles and his parents got out for a breath of fresh air in 1949.

celebrated the prince's birth, knowing that one day he would become their king.

The new parents missed many of Prince Charles's childhood firsts while they traveled. They were away when their son's first tooth appeared. They were also out of the country when he took his first steps. Charles's first word was "Nana." He said it to Mabel Anderson, the nanny who cared for him most of the time.

Charles's life was different from the lives of other young boys. At the age of four, he attended his mother's coronation. Queen Elizabeth II ascended the throne when her father died unexpectedly in 1952. She was 25 years old. Royal tradition stated that Charles should bow his head and Anne should curtsy as they entered a room where the queen was. But Elizabeth insisted that her children would not be made to do this.

Philip wanted to prepare his son for the demands of royal life. To Philip, this meant teaching young Charles to act like a man even though he was only a boy. Charles was set to have a childhood unlike most other young people would ever experience.

EXPLORE ONLINE

Chapter One discusses King Charles III's coronation. The website below goes into more depth on this topic. How is the information from the website the same as the information in Chapter One? What new information did you learn from the website?

THE CORONATION OF KING CHARLES III

abdocorelibrary.com/charles-iii

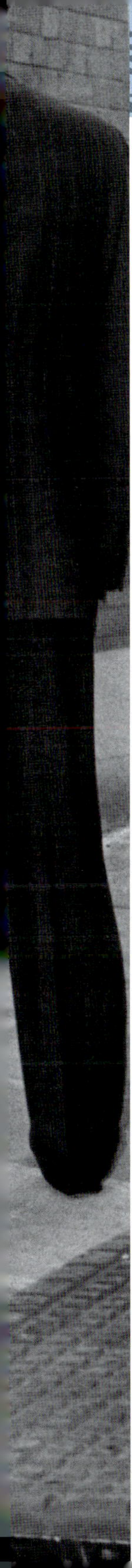

CHAPTER TWO

A LONELY CHILDHOOD

Having a private tutor for children had long been the tradition in the royal household. Charles also began his education this way at Buckingham Palace. But at eight years old, he became the first heir apparent to attend school. Philip believed that structure and discipline would make his son into a strong leader. Charles was enrolled at Hill House School in London. His first report card stated that Charles deeply enjoyed drawing and painting. But he struggled with learning math.

Prince Charles, *front*, boarded a bus to attend his sports day at Hill House School in 1957.

CHARLES AND THE QUEEN MOTHER

Charles had a special relationship with his grandmother, the Queen Mother. He often visited her while his mother and father traveled. The Queen Mother introduced young Charles to music and art. He felt like she appreciated the arts more than either of his parents did. He once told the press that his grandmother meant everything to him.

A few months later, his parents decided to send him to Cheam School in Hampshire. Philip had attended this school himself as a child. Unlike Hill House, Cheam was a boarding school. Students lived on the grounds for most of the school year. Philip worried that Charles was too sensitive. He thought that attending Cheam would toughen Charles up. But Charles did not enjoy his time at the school.

Charles and his father had a difficult relationship during these years. Charles often felt that Philip was disappointed in him. But they found common ground while enjoying nature together. On breaks from school,

Prince Charles, *center*, arrived for his first term at Gordonstoun in 1962 with his father, Prince Philip, *left*, and Captain Iain Tennant, *right*, a member of the school's board of governors.

Philip often took Charles hunting and fishing. A love of the outdoors was one of the few things they had in common.

BOARDING SCHOOL IN SCOTLAND

When Charles was 13, his parents sent him to Scotland to attend Gordonstoun. This was another boarding school that Philip had attended. Being a student at Gordonstoun was demanding. Mornings began with a run before breakfast, followed by a cold shower. Charles wanted to please his parents. But he felt lonely and homesick at Gordonstoun and was often bullied.

HIGHER EDUCATION

After graduating from Gordonstoun in 1967, Charles went to the University of Cambridge. There he appeared in many plays. He enjoyed performing onstage and speaking in front of audiences. This would come in handy for his duties as the Prince of Wales. He had been known by this title since he was nine years old. But soon he would take part in a large ceremony that would make the title official.

Called his investiture, the ceremony took place in Wales on July 1, 1969. Queen Elizabeth II presented Charles to the Welsh people as their prince at the event. To prepare, he spent a few months at Aberystwyth University in Wales. He studied Welsh history, Welsh culture, and the Welsh language.

Heirs to the throne typically went straight into the armed forces instead of going to college. But Charles graduated from the University of Cambridge with a degree in history in 1970. He was the first British monarch with a university degree.

STRAIGHT TO THE **SOURCE**

Christopher Andersen is the author of *The King: The Life of Charles III*. In his book, Andersen describes a rare bright point from Charles's time at boarding school:

> *Cast to understudy the lead role of Richard III in a school production of David Munir's* The Last Baron, *Charles stepped into the spotlight at the last minute when the star transferred to another school. . . . Since the Queen and Prince Philip were, as was so often the case, out of the country, Princess Anne and the Queen Mother made it a point to be in the audience. . . . With the exception of this and a handful of other moments that would fade into the recesses of his memory, Charles was blunt about his first five years at boarding school. "Did I enjoy it?" he would say, pausing for effect. "I loathed it."*

Source: Christopher Andersen. *The King: The Life of Charles III*. Gallery, 2022, p. 61.

CONSIDER YOUR AUDIENCE

Read the passage above closely. Write a blog post about this information for a new audience, such as your classmates. How does your post differ from the original text, and why?

CHAPTER THREE

UNIVERSITY AND THE SERVICE

While at Cambridge, Charles dated a young woman named Camilla Shand. Their relationship didn't seem to have much of a future at the time. The royal family had many expectations for the prince's future wife. One was that the woman come from a noble family. Camilla did not have an aristocratic background. With no hope of marriage, she and Charles ended their romantic relationship as he prepared to enter the military.

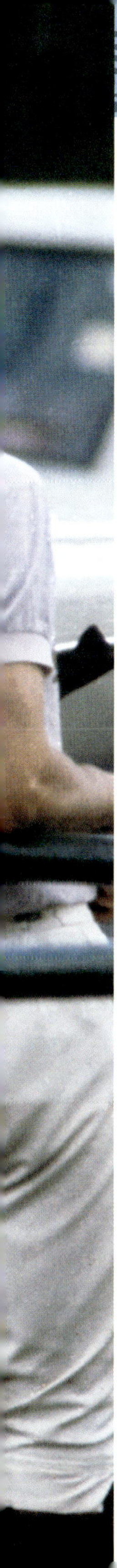

Prince Charles, *left*, spoke with Camilla Shand, *center*, after a polo match in 1972.

Prince Charles prepared for a helicopter flying lesson at the Royal Naval Air Station in Yeovilton, Somerset, England, in 1974.

Upon becoming king, Charles would be the head of the British armed services. For this reason, he wanted to take an active role in all three military branches. As a student at Cambridge, he began taking flying lessons from the Royal Air Force in 1971. After graduation, he went on to train as a jet pilot in this military branch.

When in the Royal Air Force, Charles asked if he could take part in a parachute training course for the

British Army. Some people were surprised he wanted to do something so dangerous. Charles reminded them that he would one day become the colonel-in-chief of the parachute regiment. He said he would not be able to look other members in the eye if he hadn't completed the same training they did.

He then followed in his father's footsteps by joining the Royal Navy. After attending the Royal Naval College in Dartmouth, Charles served on two frigates. He was assigned to the HMS *Minerva* from 1972 to 1973. In 1974, he moved to the HMS *Jupiter*. Charles rounded out his time in the navy by learning to fly helicopters. He ended his military

A CAPABLE PILOT

During his time in the Royal Navy, Prince Charles was part of the 845 Naval Air Squadron. He flew missions in the West Atlantic, the West Indies, and Canada. Once, while flying a Westland Wessex MK-5 helicopter, the engines failed and he was forced to make an emergency landing in a field of potatoes.

Prince Charles, *center*, stands aboard the frigate HMS *Jupiter* as it docks at San Diego Naval Station, California, in 1974.

service in 1976, returning to his duties as a member of the royal family.

THE PRINCE'S TRUST

The people of the United Kingdom had seen that Charles took his royal responsibilities seriously. Those who knew Charles described him as having a generous spirit. One of the things he liked most about being the Prince of Wales was the opportunity it gave him to help others.

Charles had received about £7,000 in severance pay when he left the Royal Navy. He used the money to establish the Prince's Trust in 1976. The charity would help young people who were struggling with problems such as homelessness, mental health issues, or trouble with the law.

The Prince's Trust has helped more than one million people since its creation. Among them were many children who faced difficulties at school. Some of these kids struggled with academics. Others, like Charles, were excluded socially. The charity has also helped young adults learn the skills needed to find a job.

AN EARLY ENVIRONMENTALIST

Charles loved spending time outdoors ever since his father introduced him to nature as a child. As an adult, he continued to enjoy the beauty of the natural environment. One of his favorite hobbies was painting scenery from his many travels. As a lover of the outdoors, he worried about the damage humans were doing to the planet.

He spoke publicly about the dangers of plastics for the first time in 1970. Few people took the threat

MAKING CHANGES

Prince Charles has taken steps to reduce his own environmental impact. In addition to installing solar panels on his homes, he has converted one of his cars to run on biodiesel. This fuel is made of cooking oil instead of gasoline. He also encourages other people to take steps to help the environment by taking shorter showers and insulating their homes with sheep's wool.

of pollution seriously back then. But in the decades since, many others have become concerned about the environment. Charles continued speaking out on the matter, including the topic in many speeches. He saw making the environment a top priority as one of the best ways to improve the world for future generations. But some people have pointed out that his own behavior does not always prioritize the environment. For example, he has traveled extensively on private jets. These luxury aircraft typically carry only a small number of passengers but release large amounts of air pollution.

STRAIGHT TO THE SOURCE

In 2019, the Prince's Trust was still going strong. Prince Charles gave a speech at the Prince's Trust Awards in London. He praised many people involved with the charity, highlighting some of what they were able to accomplish together:

> *[The Prince's Trust] has enabled us to help more than 950,000 young people. We are very nearly at the million. And I hope we can support many many more young people in the future. This year alone, the Trust will support 60,000 young people. And the wonderful thing is, currently 78 percent of young people who complete a programme through my Trust go on to achieve a positive outcome, and that again is a fantastic tribute to the fantastic people who work so hard to achieve that.*

Source: "A Speech by His Royal Highness the Prince of Wales at the Prince's Trust Awards at the London Palladium." *Royal Household*, 13 Mar. 2019, royal.uk. Accessed 29 Apr. 2024.

WHAT'S THE BIG IDEA?

Take a close look at this passage. What is the main idea of this part of the speech? What evidence does Charles provide to support the main idea?

CHAPTER FOUR

MARRIAGE AND FAMILY

Charles had always planned to marry and start a family. Because he was the firstborn son and heir to the throne, his oldest child would directly follow him in the line of succession. Charles set a deadline for himself to marry by the age of 30.

His future wife would become queen when he ascended the throne. But finding the right person was challenging. Some of the women Charles dated did not want to be in the royal spotlight for the rest of their lives. There were

In 1981, Prince Charles and Lady Diana Spencer visited the royal family's Balmoral Castle in Scotland.

always many photographers and reporters wherever Charles went. As he turned 30, he was still unmarried.

But in 1980, when Charles was 32, he began dating Lady Diana Spencer. Diana's family belonged to the British aristocracy. Charles soon invited her to meet his parents and grandmother at Balmoral Castle. This was the royal family's home in Scotland. Queen Elizabeth, Prince Philip, and the Queen Mother all approved the match of Charles and Diana.

THE MATCHMAKER

Before he met Diana, Charles had briefly dated her older sister, Sarah. But Sarah did not have romantic feelings for him. Sarah was the one who introduced her sister to the prince. When news of Charles and Diana's romance became public, Sarah told the press that she was responsible for the match.

In February 1981, the couple announced their engagement to the world. On July 29, Charles and Diana married at Saint Paul's Cathedral in London.

Prince Charles kissed Lady Diana before the crowd that had gathered at Buckingham Palace after the wedding ceremony. This royal wedding tradition dates back to 1858.

People all over the world tuned in to the royal wedding on television. More than 750 million people in 74 countries watched the event that the press called a fairy-tale wedding.

WILLIAM AND HARRY

Charles and Diana became parents on June 21, 1982. Their first son, William Arthur Philip Louis, was born at Saint Mary's Hospital. When news broke about the royal birth, people began filling the streets outside the building. Hours later, the crowd cheered as Charles and Diana stepped outside the hospital with the newest prince in his mother's arms.

THE LINE TO THE THRONE

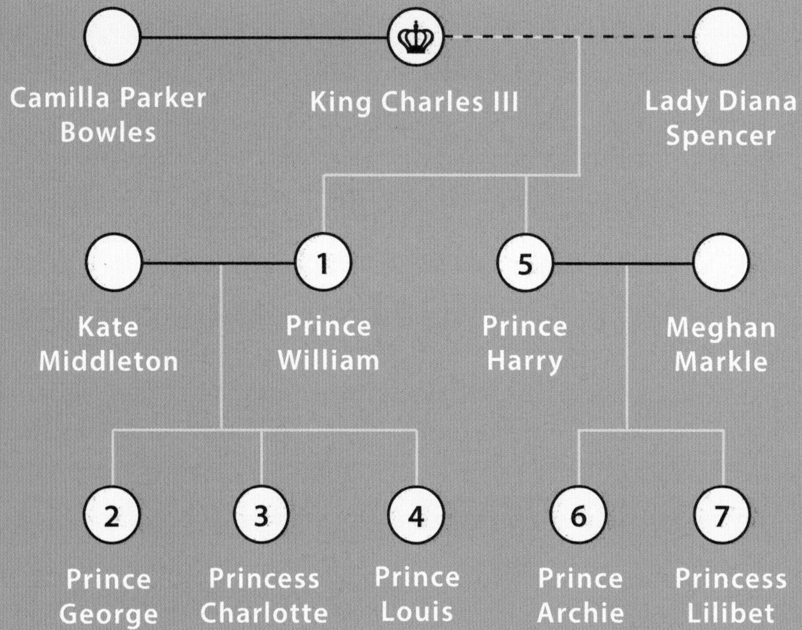

Each of King Charles's children and grandchildren has a spot in the line of succession to the throne. Study the chart above. Does anything surprise you about the order of the children and grandchildren who are in line for the throne? Why or why not?

On September 15, 1984, the couple stood outside Saint Mary's again. This time, it was to introduce William's younger brother, Henry Charles Albert David, to the world. They called the new prince Harry.

The young family received an enormous amount of attention from the media. But Diana was determined to keep her sons' lives as normal as possible. Diana had quickly become one of the most popular members of the royal family. The press was constantly trying to snap photographs of her to include with their stories. But Diana greatly limited the media's access to her children. She also made sure the family spent time together. When Diana and Charles traveled, they often took their children with them.

A DIFFERENT TYPE OF FATHER

Prince Charles was a more hands-on parent than his own mother and father had been. Charles was present when William took his first steps. When Harry was born, it was Charles who took William to the hospital to meet his baby brother. Charles also took both boys to their first day of nursery school.

DIFFICULT TIMES

Charles and Diana's marriage was not an easy one. They struggled to remain happy as husband and wife. Both had romantic relationships outside the marriage.

Charles had reconnected with Camilla Shand, now Camilla Parker Bowles. In 1992, Charles and Diana decided to separate. Many members of the royal family were upset by this decision. Queen Elizabeth did not approve of divorce. But she eventually agreed to allow the couple to end their marriage. Their divorce was made official in 1996, but they remained on friendly terms as they continued to raise their sons.

In late August 1997, tragedy struck. Diana and her romantic partner, Dodi Fayed, were in a car accident in Paris, France. Photographers had been chasing the vehicle they were riding in when it entered the Pont de l'Alma tunnel and crashed. Both of them later died at Pitié-Salpêtrière hospital.

People throughout the United Kingdom and the world mourned Diana's loss. Many were surprised by the way Charles and the rest of the royal family reacted to Diana's death. Other than a brief statement, the family said very little publicly following the deadly car accident. This angered many people.

The night before Diana's funeral, Queen Elizabeth finally broke the silence. During a television address, she explained that she and the rest of the family were grieving. She also shared that they were focusing on trying to help Prince William and Prince Harry through the terrible ordeal. William was 15, and Harry was 12. Charles was now their only living parent.

FURTHER EVIDENCE

Chapter Four discusses Charles's marriage to Diana and the birth of their two sons. What was one of the main points of this chapter? What evidence is included to support this point? Read the article at the website below. Does the information on the website support the main point of the chapter? Does it present new evidence?

TIMELINE: A LOOK AT THE LIFE AND CAREER OF KING CHARLES III

abdocorelibrary.com/charles-iii

CHAPTER FIVE

BECOMING THE KING

Like Charles, Camilla had been married and divorced. Many people believed that the reason their marriages failed was that Charles and Camilla never stopped loving each other. Much had changed since the days when they first met. Over time, the royal family relaxed its rules about the image its members presented to the public. In 1999, Charles and Camilla attended their first event as an official couple. And they

More than 30 years after they met, Prince Charles and Camilla Parker Bowles married on April 9, 2005.

Prince Charles, *left*, watched the Trooping the Colour celebration with Prince George, *center*, and Prince William, *right*, from Buckingham Palace on June 13, 2015. Trooping the Colour is a birthday celebration for the royal family.

continued their romantic relationship. With Queen Elizabeth's blessing, they married in 2005.

FAMILY ISSUES

The royal family continued to grow in the coming years. In 2011, Prince William married Kate Middleton. Kate did not come from aristocracy. William and Kate made Charles a grandfather in 2013 when their son Prince George was born. Princess Charlotte followed in 2015 and Prince Louis in 2018.

That same year, Prince Harry married American actor Meghan Markle. When Meghan's father could not attend the wedding, Charles took his place in walking the bride down the aisle. Meghan gave birth to her and Harry's firstborn, a son named Archie, in 2019. Their daughter, Lilibet, was born in 2021. Her name was Queen Elizabeth's nickname.

Harry and Meghan found their life in the royal spotlight challenging. The press was especially unkind to them and made racist remarks about Meghan. In early 2020, they announced that they were stepping down as working royals. They soon moved to the United States. Many news stories suggested a rift between the couple and other royal family members. Harry and Meghan spoke to the media about these problems, acknowledging that there had been some issues. But Charles and other members of the family said little publicly about the matter.

ENDINGS AND BEGINNINGS

On April 9, 2021, Prince Philip died at Windsor Castle. He was 99 years old. Charles left his home in

Gloucestershire to join his mother in London as soon as he learned of his father's passing. Elizabeth and Philip had been married 73 years. The loss affected her deeply.

The queen was showing signs of her own advancing age. She still attended as many events as she could. But she had far less energy than she had in the past. On September 8, 2022, Queen Elizabeth died at Balmoral Castle in Scotland. She was 96.

The people of the United Kingdom had long said "God save the queen!" as a sign of respect to the monarch. Now they would say "God save the king!" to honor King Charles. His mother's passing

NEW CURRENCY

About a year after Charles's ascension to the throne, the United Kingdom's currency took on a new look. For 64 years, banknotes had borne the image of Queen Elizabeth II. But in 2024, the Bank of England began producing banknotes bearing the image of the new monarch, King Charles III.

On September 12, 2022, King Charles III attended a memorial service for his mother, Queen Elizabeth II, at Saint Giles Cathedral in Edinburgh, Scotland.

immediately made Charles the new monarch of the United Kingdom. Nearly 70 years after he watched his mother's coronation, Charles himself was crowned on May 6, 2023.

Charles had spent most of his life preparing for this role. His title is not the only thing that has changed since he took over the throne. As king, Charles can no longer speak freely about his personal passions and opinions. He must remain unbiased on all political issues. His job as king is to support the government no matter which party is in power.

In February 2024, Buckingham Palace announced that Charles had been diagnosed with cancer. The illness was discovered in its early stages. But the king would need to step back from his royal duties for treatment. Prince William agreed to take on more public appearances and Prince Harry traveled from the United States to visit his father. Amid this unexpected challenge, the family appeared to be pulling together.

Charles vowed to continue with his state duties as he underwent treatment. The nation over which Charles now

THE OTHER KINGS NAMED CHARLES

When Charles III took the throne, it had been nearly 400 years since England had a monarch by that name. Charles I ruled from 1625 until he was convicted of high treason in 1649. He was beheaded as punishment. Charles II became king in 1660. He was known for his love of dogs. The King Charles spaniel breed, known as the English toy spaniel in the United States, was named after him.

THE BRITISH COMMONWEALTH

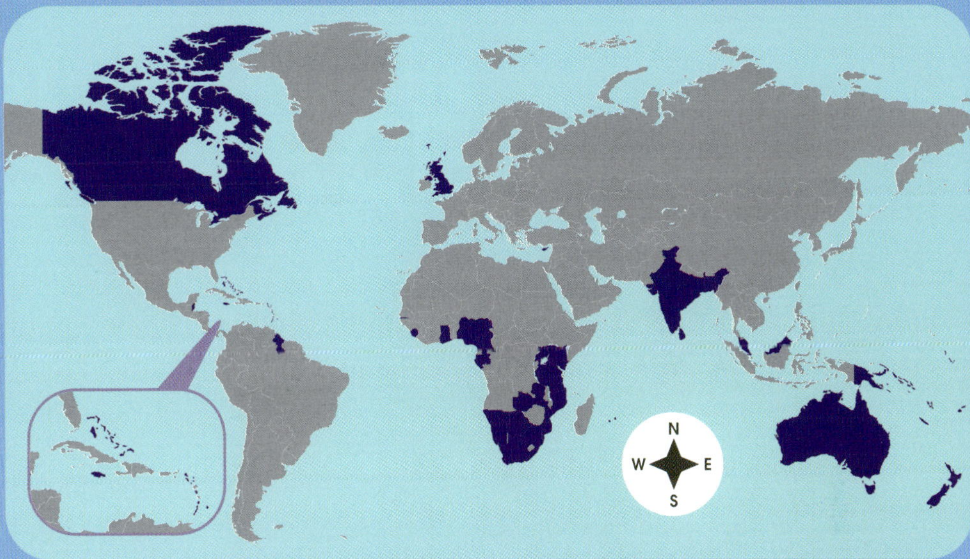

King Charles is the head of state of the British Commonwealth, which included 56 countries when he ascended the throne in 2022. What do you notice about where the Commonwealth countries are located? Can you think of one way being part of the British Commonwealth has affected daily life in these nations?

reigns has changed a lot in the years he spent preparing for the job. But his commitment to serving the people of the British Commonwealth remains his top priority.

IMPORTANT DATES

November 14, 1948
Prince Charles Philip Arthur George is born at Buckingham Palace.

1953
Charles attends his mother's coronation.

July 1, 1969
Charles formally becomes the Prince of Wales.

1970
Charles graduates from Cambridge University and enters the armed forces.

July 29, 1981
Charles marries Lady Diana Spencer.

June 21, 1982
Prince William is born at Saint Mary's Hospital.

September 15, 1984
Prince Harry is born at Saint Mary's Hospital.

1996
Charles and Diana divorce.

April 9, 2005
Charles marries Camilla Parker Bowles.

April 9, 2021
Prince Philip dies.

September 8, 2022
Queen Elizabeth II dies and Charles ascends the throne.

May 6, 2023
Charles's coronation takes place.

February 2024
Charles is diagnosed with cancer.

STOP AND THINK

Dig Deeper

After reading this book, what questions do you still have about King Charles III? Find a few reliable sources that will help you answer these questions. Write a paragraph about what you learned in this process.

Surprise Me

Chapter Two discusses King Charles III's childhood. Find three facts about his early years that most surprised you. Write a few sentences about each one. Why did you find them surprising?

Why Do I Care?

You may or may not think royalty is an outdated concept. But working royals still have prominent roles in countries such as the United Kingdom. This book describes some of the charity work King Charles has done during his life. How might he use his position as king to accomplish other positive things for his nation or the rest of the world?

You Are There

Chapter Three talks about the time King Charles III spent in the armed forces. Imagine that you were a member of the parachute regiment when Charles completed his training. Write a letter to a friend or family member describing your opinion of him taking part in the training with everyone else.

GLOSSARY

abdicate
to give up the throne

aristocratic
belonging to nobility

coronation
a ceremony for crowning a king or queen

curtsy
an act of respect marked by lowering the body and bending one's knees

frigate
a warship that is smaller than a destroyer

heir apparent
the person next in line to the throne

investiture
a ceremony to make a royal title official

severance
a sum of pay given to a person at the end of employment

succession
the line of people who will become the new monarch if the current monarch dies or steps down

treason
the crime of betraying one's country

understudy
an actor who learns the lines for a key role to play the part if needed

ONLINE RESOURCES

To learn more about King Charles III, visit our free resource websites below.

Core Library
CONNECTION
FREE! COMMON CORE MULTIMEDIA RESOURCES

Visit **abdocorelibrary.com** or scan this QR code for free Common Core resources for teachers and students, including vetted activities, multimedia, and booklinks, for deeper subject comprehension.

Booklinks
NONFICTION NETWORK
FREE! ONLINE NONFICTION RESOURCES

Visit **abdobooklinks.com** or scan this QR code for free additional online weblinks for further learning. These links are routinely monitored and updated to provide the most current information available.

LEARN MORE

Fry, Plantagenet Somerset. *Kings and Queens of England and Scotland.* DK, 2023.

Stine, Megan. *Who Was Queen Elizabeth II?* Penguin Workshop, 2021.

INDEX

About the Author

Tammy Gagne is an author and editor who specializes in nonfiction. She has written hundreds of books for both children and adults. She lives in northern New England with her husband, son, and dogs.